Being Home

Being Home

Returning to the Place We've Never Left

Reflections on the Heart of Happiness

Tom Beyer

iUniverse, Inc.
New York Lincoln Shanghai

Being Home
Returning to the Place We've Never Left

Copyright © 2007 by Thomas H. Beyer

iUniverse books may be ordered through booksellers or by contacting:

iUniverse
2021 Pine Lake Road, Suite 100
Lincoln, NE 68512
www.iuniverse.com
1-800-Authors (1-800-288-4677)

Cover Artwork by Daniel B. Holeman—www.AwakenVisions.com

ISBN-13: 978-0-595-42465-8 (pbk)
ISBN-13: 978-0-595-86799-8 (ebk)
ISBN-10: 0-595-42465-1 (pbk)
ISBN-10: 0-595-86799-5 (ebk)

Printed in the United States of America

For my family

In Deepest Gratitude To:

Jesus, Buddha, Lao Tzu, Ramana Maharshi, Jalaluddin Rumi, Nisargadatta, Ramakrishna, Kabir, Tukaram, H.W.L. Poonja, Gangaji, John DeRuiter, Adi Da, Ranjit, Mohandas Gandhi, Moses, the Dalai Lama, Ammachi, Alan Watts, Peter Davis, Saniel Bonder, Fred Sontag, Bill Whedbee, A.H. Almaas, Arjuna Nick Ardagh, Isaac Shapiro, Eihei Dogen, Shunyru Suzuki, Jack Kornfield, Eckhart Tolle, Huang Po, Ken Wilber, Robert Adams, Jean Klein, Soren Kierkegaard, Carl Jung, Frederick Nietchze, Martin Luther, Socrates, Augustine, Plotinus, Wilhelm Reich, William Blake, Walt Whitman, Rainer Rilke, Martin Buber, Herman Hesse, Chogyam Trungpa, Joseph Campbell, Ram Dass, J. and U.G. Krishnamurti, Andrew Cohen, Reb Anderson, Huston Smith, Stephen Levine, Thich Nhat Hanh, Harvey Cox, R. Richard Niebuhr, Thomas Merton, Henri Bergson, Paul Tillich, Philip Kapleau, James Redfield, Byron Katie, Peter Fenner, John-Roger, Pamela Wilson, Olon, Catherine Ingram, Adyashanti, Tony Parsons, Satyam Nadeen, Christopher Titmus, Hanuman, Meera, Francis Lucille, Douglas Harding, Ramesh Balsekar, Wayne Liquorman, Walter Starcke, Andrew Harvey, Jon Kabat-Zinn, Stephen Mitchell, Neale Donald Walsch, Thomas Cleary, Robert Aitken, Glenda Green, Achaan Chah, Barry Long, Joseph Goldstein, George Leonard, Gerald Jampolsky, Leo Buscaglia, Marianne Williamson, Alan Cohen, Robert Thurman, Andrew Weil, Joseph Forcinelli,

Anthony Robbins, Dan Millman, Deepak Chopra, Richard Bach, Don Miguel Ruiz, Wayne Dyer, George Lucas, Henry Miller, Leonard Jacobson, Paul Ferrini, Barbara Sher, Lawrence and Ardeliza Cook, Stan Arcieri and Connie Kennedy, Jane Johnston, Bob Cornelison, Beth Johnston, Elia Wise, Jim Schwartz, Pete Musto, Jerome Frisk, Steve Arnold, Paul Kelly, Zilpha and Larry Snyder, Daniel Holeman, Iasos …

… And to all my friends and relatives who teach and encourage me to share This … Thank you.

* * *

I've tried to write what I most want to read, and have spent much of my life reflecting upon. The writings are original, and they owe *much* to those listed on the previous two pages, as well as to a whole host of others, past and present. I am profoundly indebted to all those who've helped guide me; their influence underscores my desire to speak to the most common ear, in this world where divisions and divisiveness are ever so apparent.

So, in attempting to stay true to what I've learned, and to my own experience and voice, this book aims at a deep human longing—for genuine happiness, peace of mind and overall well-being. And just like us, each of the written offerings stands by itself *and* is connected to the others. One can receive them by opening at any page, or in any desired sequence—with the heart of the matter taken to heart, in whatever manner might touch us.

There is value, then, in slowly reading and re-reading what's presented here, and letting it sink in, in any instant and over time … And even as there are various topics covered, said in a variety of ways, our meeting's about one subject, really: What's alive in our very cells and in every nook and cranny of the universe, already and always. This is home, and each moment's opportunity to be here—by how we live, by how we love.

* * *

Our true home—Where everything ultimately comes from and takes place— That is floating the planets and stars, birthing each of us, breathing our breath, and sparking brainwaves and nerve impulses which activate our every function.

What a wonder, that we are one with our Creator most intimately in our hearts, where we are pulsed into existence in every instant! And as we might instinctively tap on the chest when pointing to our core, or innermost being, the Life within that's our essence has no boundaries, and exists in everyone, everywhere.

* * *

It's clear, each of us is a unique individual, with unique capabilities, ways of perceiving things, choices to make and life-directions to take; and at the same time, What we're composed of resonates with our shared origins and the greatest expanse. We're able to identify with this person who is reading this, *and* know we are much more than our names, our occupations, situations, our past and future, likes and dislikes—more than these physical, mental and emotional forms, or personas/egos.

How good, then, that even the slightest recognition of the stirring in our hearts and the Awareness looking out our eyes can enthrall us, and deeply affect the way we live and how at peace we are; especially when we're thinking or feeling in any moment cut-off from our true Nature, and buying into worries, and desires for what never really satisfies us or only seems to temporarily.

So, as we might set out on a journey of Self-discovery, we may not know we've already arrived. *Our heart's most fundamental, Source-connected truth is home,* right now, and forever after our physical passing.

* * *

In using the word "God" to refer to our Creator, our Source and Sustenance, common Origin and Destination, it's good to be aware of anything limiting our view of Who or What that is—like God is mostly "out there" and separate from us; or "He" is strictly masculine, as the supreme father figure, rule maker and judge, and partial to those who "toe the line" or believe a certain way. And for some people, God is primarily a "goddess" energy, or only found in ascended places, beyond this life, or through one messenger or group; or was only really evident years ago or only will be sometime in the future.

These are all interpretations of This that transcends every way of viewing such things—and cautionary tales, as well, of how our ideas, beliefs and convictions can tend to narrow what, in truth, cannot be ... With this in mind, I'm given to use the words "Who," "What" and "Where," "That," "This," "It" and "There" for the Totality, or Be-all-and-end-all one might point to as God. There is no gender implied in these designations, no exclusivity or anything with too rigid a meaning for the ultimately indefinable—That is deeper, more essential and beyond all definitions.

Any name for God in this book alludes to what falling into an awe-struck silence also conveys—the vastness and perfection of home, from Where we're created, are sustained by and return to—the infinite spaciousness in Which all exists.

* * *

Our essence is *most* primal and far reaching—radically more so than any belief-system, theory or insight—or anything we can say about it, hope for, or need to hold fast to or remember.

And while the question, "Who am I, *really*?" may occur as a thought, or cause some people to believe in its answer, what entices me is letting this inquiry lead to Where all thinking and believing begins and ends—Which is spread throughout the whole body, the house, the world and on and on—absorbing all of us in Reality's purest wonder and the look of our true contentment.

* * *

I sense the times in which we're living are perfect for our true well-being to be realized. When there is the greatest need to hear, there is an urgency to listen; when things seem crazy, sanity is most welcomed; and when the hardening around our hearts is so prevalent, softening is most ripe to happen.

Many of us *had* to seem lost in order to be found, had to see what doesn't work in order to know what does and go away to really appreciate being home. These are expressions of the universe in its Totality, with all Its contrasts, ironies and lessons being taught.

And a most profound learning occurs when (by whatever means and circumstances) we thoroughly investigate our *actual* nature—What pumps life into every moment of our bodily existence, and Where we dissolve back into someday—the Oneness also vibrating in grains of sand, the flow of tides, tables of wood, the wandering breeze and each seeming contradiction of appearing to be otherwise. And it is only seeming to be distant that makes it seem like we're ever returning There—to "the place we've never left."

Even if we think our heart's core-truth is just another concept or story, that's all right. We can start there, and keep reading into the irreducible meaning of it—

letting even the slightest interest and faintest hearing of all this pull us in—into what's *much* more substantial, more real and love-filled than any supposition, opinion, sentiment or ideology … If we follow this truth-telling all the way, our looking and listening give birth to understanding, and most importantly living, what an open heart radiates.

* * *

Such a miraculous mystery, that one and the same Source is beating hearts everywhere!—as every "you" and "me"—giving This a chance to experience being us and to evoke Itself in a multitude of types, and shapes and sizes.

And when we recognize the true Nature of our encounters—the Oneness underneath our diversity—we can see where compassion, generosity and true service come from, and how it is our privilege to be channels for these. We *are* these possibilities—these embodied expressions of love.

* * *

What *about* love?

My daughter Laina was born nearly four years ago, and her presence floods me with joy! I am touched beyond words and moved by how her essence connects with mine; as I am by this same sweetness I taste with my wife Minako—in the open-hearted, passionate acknowledgment of our union and the peacefulness at our core ... And this bond exists in unique fashion with Minako's son Lucas, and with my mother, father, sisters Barbara and Rebecca, brother Gary, other relatives and friends.

Every being is given life in each moment via the heart; and here, within each Source-connected pulse, is an intimacy as vast, as infinite, as God is. This is the very substance of our being—our *true* Nature. Love, then, as the heart's openness, is both Who we really are and our most fundamental and highly valued expression of This ... So, in holding one's newborn baby or the people with whom we're closest, we can sense a direct, most satisfying link to our true Sustenance and a primary reason for our being here—to incarnate love.

Or said in this way: When we open from the heart, we are quintessentially aligned with the One who is creating and embracing Herself/Himself through countless forms; and vice versa, when we recognize the whole truth about ourselves, we're naturally inclined to bring the open heart, bring love, to our various encounters ... And this can be so universal as to include all that is, or specifically manifested in "brotherly" ways, romantic, sensual and tender ways—toward our mate, our children, our parents, siblings, friends or in any circumstance and endeavor.

No matter where our affections rest, it's clear to me, the real attraction is the outpouring of love itself. This fulfills us the most and best serves the particular directions our lives take.

* * *

The current of love is like a magnet inside us; and if we can't help yielding to its pull, we are truly fortunate, truly blessed.

This is my sense: Love is about blessing—both in receiving God's grace, and reciprocating this, duplicating this, through all the open heart gives. Being irresistibly drawn to this "force-field" of God-communion is to praise it and honor it in oneself and in others. This does us the most good, and is being "lucky" in the truest sense of the word.

When we bless, we are blessed—recognizing love's preeminence in our lives, and the willingness to serve this recognition and common Origin in whatever we do and wherever we go.

* * *

Many people tend to think, feel and act in ways that have forgotten (or have never really known) the love inside them—as the truth of Who they are—and so they try to get it from people, things or experiences; often confusing it with infatuation, bodily sensations, emotional highs, consolations and peak experiences—all of which come and go, and often leave behind only a craving for more, and a dejection from never having found love's true nature.

These tendencies, to look for love in the ways we do, are what we've inherited, learned and practiced, and they're all around us in our culture. And it's my observation, when our openness is dependent on how someone makes us feel, or on things we own, our self-image or uplifting events, what we end up with is an imitation of the real thing. This is mistaking love for excitement and stimulation, attention and approval, and moments of narcissistic confirmation when we look in the mirror. As a result, we create endless strategies to get these, and try to find happiness in things like greater popularity, "people pleasing," flattery or even through others feeling sorry for us in order to get their sympathy.

It's no wonder many of us are often disappointed, frustrated, cynical and weary; we haven't realized what comes from all the way inside and satisfies the whole being in an authentic way … When our entire being *is* involved—when we're available to our heart of hearts, then any aspect of our humanity can be a passionate expression of this, and not an endless attempt to fill a void.

It's more than apparent, then, that genuine, lasting love isn't caused by, or confined to someone or something turning us on, or making us feel a certain way about ourselves. And certainly, what we long for can never be replaced by the excuses we make for our loveless ways, or playing the victim and trying to get others to pity us (for all we've suffered because of our past, or lack of opportunities, our physical appearance or poor health).

The bottom line? Real love is never found in seeking what is subject to conditioned behavior, and the fickleness of wants and circumstances—in what is transitory, unpredictable, undependable and stays only on our periphery.

* * *

Relying on any thought, feeling-state, person or situation; or thing we own, substance we take or position we attain—relying on any of these to generate love in us ignores the most vital, sustaining Power of the open heart and what is always here. And since our conditioned thinking, emotional reactions and behavior are as embedded as they are, it's good to continually go to our innermost for guidance and let this *re*-condition us. Then, we know it's not about getting a pleasant "hit" from somebody, or experience or thing, but about *being* love, no matter what we may or may not appear to get back … It's about giving way to our essence and living a life infused with it—being re-conditioned by simply and utterly settling in the Unconditional.

* * *

Until we realize the truth about ourselves, our insecurities and unfulfilled desires can run much of our lives. Even if we get what we think we want, there is often a subtle, or not so subtle dissatisfaction because our whole being isn't being fed and nourished.

Make a fist, tighten it, and feel the tension caused by this activity. This is just like our tendency to fixate on ourselves—as these individuated forms we continually try to pleasure, make more secure, work on or struggle to accept. And with this constant grasping for what we think will make us happy, and our being braced against and rejecting anything to the contrary, it's easy to see why many of us haven't discovered a true and lasting inner peace.

All this happens when we so rigidly believe our sense of "I," or "me and mine" is the extent of who we are—identifying with our "stories," or conjectures or assumptions about ourselves to the point of not seeing beyond these dramas of thoughts and feelings, habits and behavior, past or present events, our anxieties and hopes and aches and pains.

Thankfully, we can observe that we bind and limit ourselves, and in such a moment of awareness, open our tightly clenched "fist" and catch a glimpse of what's inside us. This reveals the home we may appear to leave, but never have, in fact. As far as I'm concerned, this reconciliation, this homecoming, is any life's true reward and the answer to having strayed—realizing we are already restored and have always been whole, in truth.

* * *

In looking to Where each split second of our awareness begins and flows through, this question, "Who *am* I?" comes face to face with the answer.

It's also true, many people have no interest in any of this—being preoccupied, instead, with a saga of predicaments and plans, in which hopes and dreams can be merely distant images of consolation one clings to ... And it is my experience, the more we identify with ourselves in these ways, the less likely we are to find the depth of happiness we might be seeking—even if our lives seem well-ordered and managed, and full of prominence and lofty ideals.

What's great, is the briefest truth-telling peek at the Life in our every molecule can wake us up and elicit our response—to being at home—consciously Source-connected, in love—in any instant, or non-stop for the rest of our days or for some amount of time in between.

And, as we might hear this from someone, read it in a book or through watching a video, it doesn't do us much good until we really investigate the truth for ourselves in whatever ways move us and impact us ... Who *are* we at our innermost? What is really here—as the Origin of our every heartbeat and breath, and likewise, each brainwave, and cell and beam of Consciousness looking out our eyes? … And how, then, to best live by giving way to this inquiry and its revelations?

* * *

In letting my innermost guide me, there's no problem with any changes I want to make in my personal life, and trying to prosper in every conceivable way. When I feel the need to modify eating habits, get more exercise, lose weight, put more attention on my livelihood or stay in closer touch with people, I can welcome these observations and pour myself into their actualization ... Who I am, in truth, includes and accepts my being identified as an individuated form, or persona/ego, who's free to alter any behavior or how time is spent.

Still, as my occupation, my income, my relationships, my looks or health might stay the same or get worse, or become greatly improved or even ideal—the deeper abiding remains, whether or not I'm appearing to succeed or fail at anything I do. This is always here—my essence, my heart's substance, and what to bring to any aspect of any life.

* * *

I love being conscious of my breathing, especially as it streams all the way out and then begins again, and again and again …

This is one way to experience the life-giving Energy flowing through us, so awareness of our breathing is always good, as is taking a deep breath whenever we are moved. And the only way to breathe in completely is to fully exhale first … Let go, and receiving automatically happens.

In being here, then, wherever we are, we can simply follow the inhalation and exhalation of That who is creating us—animating and transforming us—now and beyond our form, eternally.

* * *

Meditation, in the simplest and purest sense, is Awareness itself. Thus, any moment is meditation, no matter what activities we're involved in. And, we have the ongoing opportunity to be *in* the moment, which is where we always are, only now we're conscious of meeting it ... The very same can be said in this way: The heart's center is always open, and we can open to it and from it, be just like it, as we inevitably encounter any tendency in us to the contrary.

Any facet of our lives is this chance—to be present, as love—while washing the dishes, in being with family and friends, while at work, exercising, driving the kids to school, anything. In the process, we can understand the play of our thoughts, and feelings and circumstances for what they are—as useful in helping us navigate life's day-to-day journey—and more useful still, as the material we get to shine on with the light of Awareness.

How wonderful, then, that we're given the capacity to see through anything arising in mind, emotion and body (no matter how apparently problematic or confining), and identify with the Seeing itself— knowing we're *really* here, at home—Where everything is recognized to be arising out of and falling back into ... We can be attentive as This in ways often called meditation: In being quiet and still, in sensing the breath of Life, and through all an alert and inquisitive mind can look to and ask about. And we're free to let any insight, prayer, affirmation, mantra, koan, yoga or chanting accompany our truth-telling.

There are many forms by which Consciousness travels that can serve as doorways into our innermost sanctuary—countless opportunities to settle into the open heart, and to let our pondering gaze behold the One who is gazing!

* * *

Situations in and around us might seem good, might seem bad; this may never change. In fact, it's certain, there'll be both the pleasant and the unpleasant, victories and defeats. The real issue is our relationship to any occasion—What we're taken by and take with us, no matter where we go or the events occurring.

Even when circumstances overwhelm us and seem to bury all that's favorable, we can plunge further still—free-falling in God's bottomless being, Where assurance is resounding and we can't help rejoicing.

* * *

Integral to God's totality is this realm of polarities in which we live—of light and dark, birth and death, highs and lows, difficult and easy, agreement and disagreement, comedies and tragedies; the list is most immense, and for a reason ... Without the darkness, there wouldn't be anything to illuminate and transform, as each sunrise couldn't exist without the night before it also existing. In the same vein, we feel cold by the absence of heat, a cramped space by the lack of room and an open hand because of a closed one. We recognize the good guy in a story by his relationship to the bad guy, as every such tale has something to solve, to overcome—something to which a happy ending refers and has meaning.

Similarly, being kind and forgiving wouldn't stand out as much without our capacity to be resentful, have animosities and hold on to grudges ... And how else would we value love's sublimity like we do? It wouldn't feel so good, so right, if we didn't have anything to contrast it with, and didn't experience the pain of our discord and conflicts.

With this understanding in mind, we can see our tendency to take things so personally, culturally or ideologically that we feel threatened by anything we perceive will thwart our self or group interests, or might do us harm; and thus, the impulse to fight back ... And, for many of us, there is often a sense we're bracing ourselves for combat, even if we're not literally at war. In daily life, as we identify so heavily with our ego/form, "fists" can be up—trying as we might to perpetually prove and protect ourselves. In subtle or not so subtle ways, we experience being up against another, being someone who might retaliate, feel victorious or defeated—all of it.

It's clear to me, then, our Creator is giving us *many* moments to learn about differences, problems and struggles, *and* real resolution and healing—how any of our defensive and cruel tendencies can defer to the comforting calm at our depths.

* * *

When I live based on what I know is true, all is well, even if the world seems, at times, to be harsh, unfair and full of chaos. And my primary devotion can always be my heart's truth, even if I need to stand up for myself or defend my loved ones.

When I feel some person or situation is wrong, I have the great opportunity to act with a strength that is simultaneously considerate of Who a person *is*, deep down. If I get offended, lose my temper (or someone with me), my essence is still here, still beckoning. Hearing this may occur in an instant, or after a period of time—cluing me in to how I contribute to the world's ills by being close-minded or mean-spirited myself. And if I lash out at anyone, I get to see if I am merely mimicking the qualities of the people I'm blaming, galvanizing opposition toward me and creating further backlash and trouble for everyone.

And let's be real: I may be living by the highest wisdom, and someone could still take a punch at me, or break into my house to steal things or do my family harm … What then? There's no doubt, I would completely guard us all in whatever ways were needed; *and*, in the name of love and its Source, any self-defense returns, as quickly as possible, to the peace I treasure in being home.

* * *

For many of us, part of being alive is about having beliefs, in the form of convictions, that can manifest in all kinds of ways—like speaking up for what we feel is right and doing what we're able to improve the world. We can work to decrease hunger, or the abuse of children or environmental destruction; or stand up to a local bully, a corrupt regime or hypocrisy and injustices of any sort. These and many other issues are worth addressing, and people will be drawn to them in their own manner.

In my view, *how* we go about "righting wrongs" is ultimately the most important consideration … We make the world an even more loveless place by being this way ourselves, no matter what our causes may represent or how good they may seem.

Be wary, then, of any person or group proclaiming they walk on the highest "moral" ground, especially if this keeps people embittered, intolerant and worsens adversarial conditions … It's always important to ask ourselves, "What is genuinely worthy and *truly* effective in helping us better our world, and what do we want to be left with after any changes are said and done?"

* * *

What's going on in places like the Middle East, and has spread to other parts of the world, indicates how extreme the identification with one's personal or group point of view and its dogma can be. When, "I'm right and you're wrong" vendettas gain such unresolved momentum over time, and those involved are *so* entrenched in their side's story and the justification of their grievances, the animosity easily becomes "hair-triggered" and full of martyrdom. And with more people's willingness to kill and die for their beliefs, we see the results we do—as news footage, in our face immediately on TV or the Internet ... And because of this easy access to information, any violence resulting from the taking of sides can quickly erupt in other places.

So, in terms of the relationship between Israel and Palestine, for example (and what continues to figure in to conflicts in other places), it's most important to look at What their cultures are founded on, as Jews and Muslims, and forever links them. Therein lies the key— to each accepting the other's right to exist, and to finding a mutually agreed upon home for all their people; and resolving these issues depends on a relentless appeal to the *heart* of both Judaism and Islam—relying on it and abiding thus.

Only when God's *all-pervading spirit*, all-pervading love, is valued more than a rigid attachment to specific territory, and any justification for retribution (not to mention any delusions of ideological superiority)—only then can the feuding and its bloodshed cease, lands be shared and sovereignties respected. This shift will require strong leadership and peacekeeping resolve, with the courage to speak what both groups, and any others trumpeting their causes must be willing to heed— the holy principles of the wisdom-lineage they have in common.

Likewise, between Christians, Jews and Muslims, and the United States, its allies, and the Arab world, in general (and anyone and anybody, actually): When we really live according to the *essence* of our spiritual forefather's teachings, and so honor their significance and similarity, then any vestiges of self-righteousness, fanaticism, intolerance and tyranny naturally give way to the real heritage of us all—the *one* God resonating in each of our hearts and expressed most essentially in our love.

* * *

When we so adamantly believe we're on the side that's right, to the point of refusing to empathize in any way with the other's plight, then being defensive in our stance and retaliatory in our actions can control us. And if our reactions become violent, then revenge seeking and continued violence often occur.

Of those toward whom we might feel anger, or seem easy to despise: Can we give both their actions *and* ours a thorough enough look-see, in order to understand what caused such reactive emotions, and how we may have perpetuated any "sword rattling" or even created more enemies by our behavior? ... While affirming the right to defend ourselves, can we usher any situation inside to the realization of Who we are, *really*? Then, we might have a chance to work things out, rather than continually fanning the flames of rancor, contempt and distrust.

It's clear to me, we're being called to look as deeply as we can inside ourselves—deeper than ideology and causes—deeper than animosity, hurt, personal or group history, everything. This is our challenge, and the opportunity for real creativity and problem solving. And this will only happen when it does—when our innermost being is most highly valued by enough of us and allowed to have the final say ... This is the voice of our true conscience, and our willingness to tell the whole truth about ourselves and to live according to that.

I'm convinced that abiding by our truth-telling has the potential to relax the most complex tensions, and render *great* help in finding the necessary compromises to any situation … Now's the time!—to be honest enough about ourselves, about our core-Oneness, *and* our arrogance and stubbornness and how we try to force our will on others. Now's the time to acknowledge our pining for this—for an honesty of conscience that will seep through the walls we build around our hearts, and for an adherence to our common Source and the love flowing from There. I see this hunger everywhere—in people's eyes, in people's faces, in our speech and actions.

* * *

How lucky we are when the pain of our cold-heartedness is enough to "break our hearts," and thaw us out with the warmth of tenderness always deep inside.

* * *

In lending an ear, I can hear the voice in all of us, crying to be listened to, crying to be heard.

In looking closely, I can see our eyes longing to see What's really here, longing to be treasured.

And with all of this, I can feel us aching to find ourselves at home, in peace.

* * *

IV

Wanting anything to stay in its present form or state goes against the current that naturally flows—as everything, everyone, every experience, thought, emotion or perception *is*, in each moment, forming and fading, arising and passing, however rapidly or slowly.

But not to worry—for even though rain and river, spring and sweat, tears and ocean are different tastes, they are all still water—all the same Substance, from the same Source.

* * *

We live in a world filled with our humanness—with all the emotions we share, and the situations which impact us and touch common threads … Being human includes our vulnerability, in all its undeniable rawness. Anyone who's been terrified and traumatized when his or her child is missing, or who has experienced the cruelty of war or the loss of a loved one, knows what I'm talking about—how our lives are susceptible to the most shattering blows.

Simultaneously, this realm has a home Wherein thoughts, feelings and beings of all kinds come and go; Where birth and death, elation and tragedy, tribulation and trial have their place as natural contrasts. This includes both our limited, earthly life-span *and* our everlastingness.

These two "worlds" may appear different on the surface, and in their size and shape; but if, in any moment, we follow our truth-wonder all the way, There's the merging of every dimension.

* * *

Fear, sadness and anger are part of the entire spectrum of emotions, and go with the territory of being human and the desire to secure and prolong our physical life; they are most natural.

Fear grips us, then, when we feel threatened, and shudder at the possibility of being seared by any pain or losing our bodily form altogether ... And when there is great disappointment or loss, especially with a loved one's death, a sorrow can excavate us down to a gut-level need to mourn ... And we can easily take offense and become indignant, when our personal or collective identity wants to defend itself against a threat, or when we view something as unfair or unjust.

In acknowledging these aspects of our humanity, we know it's best to not suppress any anxiety, melancholy, despair or upset; nor deny being terror stricken, full of grief or enraged. All these exist for a reason, and enable us to be how we are at our core—the infinity in our heart of hearts—where that much space is given for every inch of us to reside.

* * *

There will always be the inclination to care for our bodies and those near and dear to us. In looking after our loved ones, we do everything we can to ensure their safety and their physical, mental and emotional well-being—taking all necessary precautions, especially for our children, who may not be able to for themselves. This is one of the great opportunities in our being alive—to really care for others, our families especially.

We know there are dangerous situations in which we can find ourselves, and there is natural concern when something might be wrong. So, we instinctively steady a child's shaky steps, and securely hold on to anything with weight to keep it from falling on us. And, if we're smart, we heed all appropriate warnings about any risky endeavor and diligently apply every safety feature possible.

And the truth is, at any moment, the body, the mind and any person or thing can disappear. There are no perfect safeguards for anyone's health and protection. Anything can happen at any time, and this may be something nerve-racking, life threatening or prone to cause panic; it is part of being on this earth in these very fragile and finite forms … No one knows how much time each of us has here, and while we might want a guarantee for our security and longevity, this is simply not available. We do all we're able, and then …

Then, it's time to *completely* trust God ... Our vulnerability and physical mortality are, in fact, the means of this incentive and our greatest solace— surrendering to the Life that's living us, and Where we return when our current stay in this world is up.

* * *

Catastrophic events of nature and incurable diseases can affect us differently than dealing with people who do hurtful things. Whatever we experience regarding human acts we consider vicious or evil may vary from our reaction to an earthquake, a flood, cancer or AIDS. And there is no getting around it, people are capable of the worst possible things, and the most terrible natural disasters and illnesses do happen.

Nevertheless, as we might think some of our acts are wrong or evil, and "acts of God" are not, the heart's truth can still be found shedding its light and giving us clarity—on how to see others (even the worst among us), and be OK with our inevitable passing, however it's caused.

Our appearance as this organism is a slice of time in the continuum of our true Self—a blip on the "screen" of Who we are, and a tiny portion of the spectrum of Light that illuminates us. However it occurs, the ending of anyone's particular "movie" may be sudden, unexpected, or after a more extended visit in this realm full of destructive possibilities … What saving Grace that whatever takes place, Who we are, in truth, goes on and on, as we have since the beginning of it all. What a blessed opportunity to be aware of the "big picture" while our present form's alive!

* * *

This is how I see the circle of Life: Forms are continually being created, lived and breathed for a time, and then cycled back into that same One, eternal power of Consciousness through which we are aware in every moment … Thus, in facing the inevitability of our death, we come upon a fuller sense of our Being—the destination programmed in these body "clocks" that are made, tick away and eventually stop; and when this happens, the Timeless is met.

Just the same, grief at someone's dying is a most natural occurrence. When we're close to a person and he or she dies, it *is* sad. It's my sense, that missing someone like this is meant to tenderize us, open us, so love can thoroughly infiltrate our lives, saturate us, and help our relationships mean even more to us … Then, we might finally acknowledge the love that's everywhere, and inviting us to be evermore just like it.

So, in being with a loved one's death, or the prospect of our own, we are humbled by What all forms are at the mercy of, and actually consist of. And knowing the current body-mind's time may be up at any time puts any day-to-day concerns in proper perspective. This helps us recognize what's really important and to just let every aspect of our lives free-fall and settle—into our true, undying Condition.

* * *

Thoughts and emotions can seem, at times, to grab at us, "pinch" us, and over time leave scars. And for many people, these are ones of uneasiness, loss, disappointment and bitterness—which can cause a person to shut down and be armored way too much, for way too long.

This is precisely what Awareness is suited for—to take aim and meet, shine on and penetrate *all* the way through any layers of mind, and feelings and events—rendering them transparent to the Incandescence and this no-thing-ness of vast clarity.

* * *

There's a tendency in all of us to push away anything painful, to cling to the opposite, and seek distractions to escape the emotional impact of what we're going through … This is understandable, seeing that when an individualized being appears, there's an impulse to protect that one and look after its survival.

Yet even if our lives are not directly at risk, and our basic needs are taken care of, the same thing can be taking place—trying to avoid any uncomfortable thoughts, or feelings or circumstances, and seeking pleasure or relief in consoling experiences … But avoidance always has a price to pay, as the refusal to face what we won't holds a more extensive suffering than what we might try to suppress or forget; both in the lingering tension around what we're avoiding, and in the futile search to make it go away or be other than it is.

When we take even an instant to actually look, and bring to light what we're hesitant to, it's just like the scientist who peers into something with a powerful enough microscope, and sees that the innermost of *everything and everyone* is nothing but space, pure energy, where there is nothing solid or defined. This is a fact, not just an idea or theory … Therefore, in terms of our anxiety or insecurity, and all the ways we seek to relieve it, repress it or discharge its energy: best to just be with it, and really look into the actual substance of any distressful thought;

and with our emotions—to completely feel them, and all the shaking, numbness and paralysis that might occur—including being pierced to our depths, and facing the destined vanishing of these bodily forms (which is what every fear is ultimately about, and what our contrivances and best laid plans can never make go away).

This is what the smart ones have always done—die to mis-identifying oneself, by letting go to the truth of Who we are—to What lives us, and can take us back in the blink of an eye—Where there is no such thing as security as a persona might want for itself ... Without trying to change anything, escape what we're feeling or be rid of any sensation; and without dramatizing the stories of our emotions, or lashing out at anyone we might blame for them, we can meet and keep meeting What is really there and provides the greatest security of all. Here, even our non-existence is in Those hands and no-thing to resist at all.

* * *

Our thoughts and feelings spontaneously arise on their own; it's how Life is speaking through the language of genetic coding, our upbringing, the culture in which we live and the choices we've made. Wisdom tells us, then, to simply let what comes up in mind and emotion come up.

And at any time, it's also good to see if we are buying into any limited version, or story, of who we are. One such common tale is full of egos struggling to "make it," and situations to win over, rise above or else be defeated and fail … For many of us, if we read between the lines, there lie conditioned beliefs of not being good enough; and even if we presume we are, we might suffer in comparison to those we imagine are better.

These self-views can have a lot of ups and downs, and back and forth to them: "I'm a success, I'm a failure; I'm smart, I'm dumb; I'm beautiful, I'm ugly; a winner, a loser; clever, dull; worthy, unworthy" and so on. What we don't like about ourselves is often made into something we're either resigned to and dejected about, or think we must willfully overcome.

Even in terms of discovering our true Self, we might try and be more focused, or more proficient at meditating, remembering the truth, doing good deeds, praying more often and so on. Or, we might feel the need to be stronger in our faith, to get rid of apparent obstacles or purify our energy. It's good, actually, that all this happens, to see if there really *is* something necessary to do or some place to get to, if only we improve ourselves enough—to see if there is anything essential to seek we don't already have. Likewise, it's useful to look at what *really* happens if we don't seem to get anywhere, or when we supposedly fail and remain full of our human frailties.

It's clear to me, trying to be Who we are, or attain some special, unchanging feeling-state we might think our core-truth is all about, is unnecessary effort and the "spinning of wheels" of many a spiritual seeker. And can't most of us relate to this—believing in one moment we're "awake," and how confused and unhappy we are at other times, convinced we have to practice harder to regain what we imagine we've lost? In reality, all emotional states, ideas about ourselves and varieties of mental activity come and go *in* the totality of our Being—our apparently enlightened times and the seemingly unenlightened ones arising and passing in This—that encompasses everything, stands free and witnesses everything—all our thinking we're evolving and all our thinking we're not.

* * *

At times, we may be intentionally contemplating our true Nature and our mind-forms will reflect this; or a thought or a feeling may pop up from out of nowhere about our core-truth, amid whatever we're engaged in. Any kind of mental activity can arise in any moment— some of it might be about our essence, and in other instances we could be focused on a particular situation, like an upcoming decision to be made or problem to be solved ... And let's face it, sometimes our thinking will sound noisy, sometimes more quiet, sometimes agitated, sometimes tranquil; appearing positive and supportive in certain occasions, or more critical, bothersome and even tyrannical in others. Numerous variations of these thought-tendencies can occur in the course of one day, not to mention a lifetime.

All that's taking place in mind and emotion is in the "ocean" of our Being, containing every size and shape of wave, every choppy sea and calm one, muddied water and the most pristine; or to use another analogy, it's all in the "sky" which is broad enough for every kind of weather, be it stormy or sunny. This is Who we really are, Consciousness itself, the medium through which all is passing—including how we identify with the "wave" feeling separate from, or at odds with the ocean, or the "cloud" not realizing the abundance of air that floats it.

How wonderful, then, to be aware of This, for an instant or as often as we can. And whether or not this seems to be happening in any moment, our awakening points deeper—to the Substratum, the certitude, of What's dwelling in our every cavity and very marrow, no matter what we're thinking or how we may appear to be ... So, this recognition of our Source-connected essence may correspond to a specific feeling, or may not. Thoughts and feelings come and go, while the Vastness enveloping it all, permeating it all, remains constant—regardless of any "waves" tossing us about or appearances "clouding" our view of the sky.

And to look at this in yet another way: We can see our thoughts and feelings coming from the fertile ground of imagination, from the "play of Consciousness"—that allows us to manifest in this world what we will ... And don't some of us love to dream up intriguing life stories, devise elaborate strategies for success, solve problems (even made up ones), win at games, and create things which pique our interest and stimulate our senses? Any piece of art on canvas, in print, as music, written fiction, in a film or just in our heads, can be forms of fascination we adore or detest, that engage us and give rise to feedback and interaction. This is part of Life's "theater." The question is, how caught up are we in believing the sounds, and dramas and comedies of mind are all there is to reality?

It's good, therefore, to understand the power of our mental projections, and how each of us relates to things through the filter of our individual or group storyline. And as we read into any of our mind's activity (be it apparently fictitious or factual, frivolous or necessary) there is, underneath it all, our intrinsic Nature to marvel at and proclaim ... If it seems we have to keep investigating This to even glimpse It, so be it. How lucky we are to be moved in such a way, and to inquire into and *via* the eyes of our present and eternal Perfection! How lucky we are to act in the "play," and appreciate it from this vantage point.

* * *

Wisdom tells me: Let the mind think, it will anyway. Let any feelings arise, the body tense and the ego-I be—they will anyway. All these things will happen *and we are home*, where the heart rests and all the necessary room is provided.

* * *

Whenever there's a sadness coinciding with someone's serious illness or death, I can let myself be completely sad without trying not to be; the same with any fear regarding my certain passing … Everything is allowed in—every bit of heaviness, or despair or horrifying possibility. Even if it seems like a dark cloud weighing a ton, I can let any sorrow or anxiety rain on me in a complete downpour, with nothing to stop whatever's washing through me.

The same with someone, or any frustrating situation that has pushed my buttons, caused me pain or let me down; it's best to open to anything associated with the event—giving access to any mental image of what's disturbing me and making me mad, and letting the fiery energy run through my toes, fingers, scalp, groin and belly.

Freely allowing and completely feeling what is, is how we are in our inner spaciousness. Even as we might be conditioned to resist or deny the unpleasantness of any fear, sorrow or anger, it's OK—as *any* emotion, or resistance or denial of it can be met by our truth-telling revelation: We *are* this

Vastness containing it all—that's more open than anything.

* * *

Admitting any of our dilemmas, distress or turmoil is a sound way to be in a human body-mind, and there is value in someone like a therapist or a teacher to help us with that. It could also be a friend who is there to simply listen and be supportive with what we're going through.

I also know people who have been in therapy for years, with no greater degree of happiness to show for it. There can be a wallowing in one's "stuff," as if fixating on it was an end in itself; the same with catharsis and being hooked on the energy of venting emotions. Both often coincide with endless hoping: "If only I could better understand my past and find the beginning of my dis-ease, or cry enough tears and fully release my repressed fear or anger, I'd finally be at peace."

Therapy can be a perpetual and tiresome reciting of a saga, even if it's about "getting it all together" or wanting to feel more harmonious. And as many of us have experienced, this often translates to chronically seeking newer and better techniques to fix ourselves— always with a more evolved place to get to, and greater breakthroughs and self-esteem to be had.

It's true, discovering the reasons for one's difficulties may be useful for some of us, and perhaps our lives will improve in certain ways because of a therapeutic process—adding clarity to the choices we make and the directions we take … Perhaps, our therapy will help in understanding what emotions we've locked up inside, and how we can put our minds more at ease and better treat our relationships, rather than sabotaging these by being our own worst enemy.

Still, it's plain as day to me, that even if we have completely dissected our past and are letting our feelings out, and even if we have taken firm control of our life and are no longer plagued by self-doubt, there is something *much* more beneficial to realize—much more than any interpretation of the past, hope for the future or discerning our patterns can provide … And when we dive into even a "drop" of this awakening and let it trickle through our pores, everything takes on a new light. As I see it, this is what truly helpful therapy facilitates, even if we continue to experience our wounds or need to deal with issues.

* * *

In the movie, "A Beautiful Mind," the protagonist (John) had a type of schizophrenia, which caused him to see and actually interact with certain people who didn't really exist, except in his head. A long story short, he was finally able to understand these illusions for what they were, and thereby stand free of the problems posed by mistaking his imaginary world for reality … Being with our thoughts and feelings is the same thing: We don't have to believe they're giving us the complete picture of ourselves.

And not only was John not buying into his hallucinations (by knowing they weren't real), he was also not fighting against them. For a while, he was resisting them, trying to make them disappear; this was just another form of the conflict causing him difficulties. Similarly, when we presume our mental activity and our feelings totally define who we are, there's a tendency to struggle with our thoughts, and emotions and sensations—trying to reject the bad (seemingly "unenlightened") ones, while wishing we had better ones.

I loved the parts of the movie, then, when the illusionary characters were floating in and out of a scene, and John knew they didn't have power over him anymore. He could accept them and peacefully coexist with them … As he was doing what he was doing—being focused on his work, or his relationship with his wife or whatever—everything was essentially all right, whether the make-believe people were appearing or not; he knew the figments of his imagination were just that … We can relate to the play of mind in the same way—seeing that who we are is deeper-seated and further-extending than any of the thinking popping up in there.

* * *

For some of us, there is a stigma of shame in admitting to ourselves or our loved ones that we may need mental or emotional help. It's good to be honest like this, and know we all feel weak, confused, disturbed and tormented for whatever lengths of time we do—that we can go through periods of feeling helpless, even worthless, and in need of assistance in whatever ways we're moved to find it.

For some of us, this may be through counseling or therapy alone, or in conjunction with some type of medication (which, it's obvious to me, is necessary for some people). And chemical, nutritional or lifestyle imbalances, and any other related physical and medical issues do exist; so it's good to address them.

Of equal importance as far as I'm concerned (and what any good therapy enables), is to stand in place, and not deny or run from any thought or emotion … When we can no longer escape being shame-ridden, fearful and despondent, things actually become much clearer, much freer. Our normal defenses are down, and the chinks in our armor exposed; and what we've previously used to avoid our feelings can no longer keep us from being like we are at home, and cradling our *every* part.

* * *

How good it is to feel in and as the whole body as we breathe—in our belly, genitals, legs and feet, solar plexus, chest, arms, throat and head—all over.

In this or any moment, we are being breathed!—our every breath coming from out of nowhere—Where all inhaling begins, exhaling disperses, and nothing *Real* ever leaves us.

* * *

When we're in pain because of an illness or an injury, it's most natural to do everything we can to relieve it; the same with any discomfort our loved ones might be experiencing. And, there *is* pain which can't be relieved, or only partially so, or only on some days and not others … We can explore any and all means to deal with any hurt—medically, pharmaceutically or through more natural means, *and* be willing to let it be.

I know some people will say, "Oh, I have tried to accept my worsening physical condition and that hasn't worked." What to do, but allow those feelings as well, and to feel free to fight an ailment in any way we want. Letting be means just this—we don't have to put on a smiley face, and try to like what's occurring and not do anything about it. For any of us, dealing with a disease or a disability may be our main concern, and where we direct a great deal of energy and attention … Likewise, if a person is starving, first things first, find food!

And the fact remains, our ailing may continue no matter what we do, and may last a long time and even be terminal … Pain *is* real, sickness and death undeniable; and it is Life encouraging us to fully meet any experience, and peer into it with our most truth-exposing "microscope." I'm continually shown this is the best way to live, whether we're bodily healthy, or dealing with an illness or an injury.

Thus, there are testimonials with a similar tone: "Before my health crisis began, I was so wrapped in things, and unable to see beyond the world I assumed everything revolved around. And while I was sick, the whole ordeal often felt unimaginably hard to bear ... At some point it became evident, that Life was crying out for me to *stop* and be 'unwrapped'—be nothing but vulnerable, wide open and given to the 'Be-all-and-end-all,' given to God ... What a blessing, that came disguised in order to garner my undivided attention, and unveil What I've come to cherish most of all."

* * *

As far as praying for good health, a more peaceful world or the happiness of our loved ones—any such yearning is welcomed like a long-lost friend into where the truth be told, and the greatest help is unceasingly given ... The same with facing adversity, feeling weak or stuck, or when our efforts have fallen short, plans haven't materialized or we seem at our wit's end—all these are occasions when our heart's home is *most* inviting, and where it's always OK to fall to pieces.

* * *

Like many people, I prayed a lot for the right intimate relationship to occur in my life. As it so happened, this came true, as did my desire to be a father.

But why have the most suitable partner (or anything for that matter), save for an intimacy with one's most *vital* interest? … If I think any personal relationship is going to give me something by itself, so I'm just clinging to the good feelings another supposedly gives me or so I won't feel lonely, then I'm in for a rude awakening. And most of us experience this letdown when we find out that even a seemingly perfect match can't deliver all we thought she or he would. While we might go through this, what we often do is deny it, look to distract ourselves from it, merely put up with the other person or try to find somebody else.

And how easily we can fool and frustrate ourselves, when we expect to find true, enduring love solely through physical and emotional highs, and someone whose primary role is to stimulate us, fuel our attraction or "meet our needs." When these are valued the most, what's of incomparable worth waits to be met.

* * *

It's a wonderful part of the human experience to keep our intimacies vibrant, and never let them grow stale. The best way to do this, I'm convinced, is through endlessly renewing the vow to our deepest-reaching bond. This is the real "work" of any relationship—seeing any moment as an opportunity to *be* the open, listening heart— transparent to our innermost qualities of honesty and trust, patience, tolerance and forgiveness ... Our relationships, then, are continually blessed by continually blessing them, served best by being home—by valuing this the most and letting *everything* settle in there.

And, as we might pray for the right person to come into our life, what are we up to in the meantime? While seeking for a partner to love supremely, can we see that our Supreme love is presently here? In being "won over" by This and living accordingly, the real prayer is already answered, however our sentiments for someone (or his or her feelings toward us) might fluctuate through moods, and circumstances and desire.

Perhaps, someone we've already met or the person we're currently with is indeed the "right one." If we find this out, or truly feel the need to look for a different "significant other," best to let the partnership flourish in the only way it really can.

* * *

What do we *really* want? What are we doing things for? This limited time here, how do we want to spend it?

* * *

For the longest time I've had a basic curiosity: Why are we here? When we get out of bed every morning and for the rest of the day, why do what we do and for what ends? When these kinds of questions are alive in us, the consideration of what brings real happiness naturally lends itself.

Perhaps to make a decent living, and survive as best we're able are all any of us wants. Or maybe we're seeking to have more money and luxury; to be smarter, more successful, admired and popular; have perfect health, security and safety; greater status and power; the ideal partner and family; a fancier house; the most desirable body; the ultimate sexual experience; better drugs, or creative or spiritual highs; longer leisure, with more engaging hobbies and entertainment; greater physical strength, energy and longevity; a calm mind or more profound and inspirational experiences.

Any of these desires has a place in this world. They express the wide range of our embodiment, perpetuate our species, keep our stories full of dramatic twists and turns and the intrigue of wanting someone or something. And we do enjoy a good story … The ones I especially love help us get to the *core* of any story—that help us uncover and stay versed in our heart's true meaning, exuberance and peace.

* * *

While taking care of basic needs like food, shelter, health, intimacy, family and security, if we're not looking out the window of our true abode—knowing this, treasuring this—then no house we inhabit, or lifestyle we covet is ever lavish enough, glamorous enough, prestigious enough or pleasures us enough.

We can all relate to this: either lamenting over not getting what we want, or fulfilling our desires and remaining out of touch with our contented depths. Still, we go on seeking—sometimes for the same things, sometimes for different things—perhaps with more elaborate and intricate strategies, while coping with the weariness of never quenching our real thirst.

It's good to see, then, how we romanticize and live in make-believe for what we think will satisfy us through and through, and good to be dis-illusioned by this. This, to me, is Divine disappointment: the Grace in finding out what can never really "do it" for us, *and* that even these misguided attempts are part of our Self-discovery— conceding what a truly fulfilling way of being isn't, in order to know full well what it is.

* * *

It's so human to get caught up in persistent worry about the bad things that might happen, and stressed over the possibility of anything thwarting our self-interests. And, there's a common tendency to believe in those thoughts and feelings, and let them dictate our behavior—even getting angry when things go wrong or when we don't get our way.

Doesn't this sound familiar in whatever variation is true for us? "If I don't hurry up and get this done (whatever it is), I can't rest, I won't look good; or worse yet, I'll lose my job, where I live and end up on the street." Or, "If I don't pursue things with enough intensity, I won't get the pleasure, respect and admiration I crave."

Or any of this? "If only I had a more important vocation or avocation, did something extraordinary, were famous, better looking, or more clever or rich, I'd finally be free of self-doubt and feel successful and secure." Or, "If only I could find the perfect partner, or teacher, or were more mindful, inspired or had a stronger faith, I'd finally be at peace, I'd finally be happy." … Thus, the wheel of fear and desire spins, and never finds a way out of its inherent discontent.

So, when we're living as if we're being chased or are chasing something, this is the perfect time to *stop*, be conscious of the breath of Life sustaining us, and exhale and let go in There ... Then, there's no problem taking care of our business without the busy-ness taking charge of us. We're home; and this truth-telling is reminding us we're *always* here, and thankfully, stopping us from believing otherwise—even as we're active, venturing forth and doing what we do—including overcoming obstacles, and all that goes along with accomplishment, success or their opposites.

* * *

What worth is it to become anyone or accumulate anything, without living where one's most valuable treasure is?

This is not an ideal spiritual state to attain, program of self-mastery requiring mandatory steps or esoteric practices, nor the exclusive property of anyone or anything demanding allegiance or sworn oaths ... Even greater insight, enthusiasm or thinking we're more "evolved," doesn't carry any weight or have anything at stake in our innermost sanctuary.

* * *

While we might refuse to admit it, there can be a tendency to think we're not good enough—not smart, or impressive, adventuresome or worthy enough; creative, assertive, revered or pious enough. Or else we might feel we're any of these things and must work at all costs to maintain them. No wonder we're exhausted or disappointed to the extent we are … When we make the body-mind-persona into an icon, and try to perfect it above all else, we're imagining there's a real prize in all the places this can't be found. How perfect that we fail!

What's great, is our core-truth always *is*—in the ordinary, everydayness of our lives; and realizing this doesn't depend on having extraordinary abilities or powers. Thank goodness … We don't have to get "ahead," avoid falling "behind," or look or sound a certain "spiritual" way to be Where we are already whole and complete. And equally and thankfully so, one's ego-I identification needn't be overcome or overthrown, only its limits understood and accepted as such.

Thus, as we put our attention on the things we do— our health and fitness, our families, our jobs and financial situations, the environment, community affairs and so on—it's even the tiniest kernels of our heart's truth, the ones containing love's effulgence, that bear the most nourishing, best tasting fruit in whatever field they're planted in.

* * *

I notice people can be happy when circumstances are good or not so good, and people can be *un*happy when circumstances are good or not so good. Those who might appear to "have it all" are often in a malaise, brought about by the failure of any kind of ambition, accumulation and self-importance to deliver the real goods.

In contrast to this, people experiencing difficulties or those who are handicapped in some way, can still exude a warmth and serenity even amid unrest and what appears unlovable.

And let's be honest: We are fortunate if we're not preoccupied with where our next meal is coming from, or whether we'll have shelter tonight—lucky if we're not in the middle of a war torn land, or beset by the severest kinds of strife.

And, it is equally true and an even greater blessing, that if we are going through hard times or in places besieged by trouble, this is the perfect opportunity to look into the well of our being and find our true Sustenance still feeding us there … Every moment *is* this opportunity—to tell the whole truth and to choose to live accordingly.

* * *

VI

There's a teaching voice speaking from What is prior to any experience, and echoes through all that's arising and passing. Hearing this doesn't require extrasensory perception, and isn't limited to a certain type of event. There's no right kind of moment to cause the attracting of my attention, nor can this pull be measured by any special confirmation, apparent progress, or made less by any of my shortcomings.

What inhabits me and What I'm immersed in, is so, right now and without end! And recognizing This is not about getting more likable thoughts or moods, or a different, gleeful face to put over a sad face. I'm not becoming "higher" or "holier" than I was before; and if I'm ever deluded in thinking I am, well, this is just another piece of fiction to be seen for what it is.

* * *

Consider any night's sleep and what happens the following morning:

Whether we've slept a long time or a short time, had pleasant dreams or not so, the nothingness of slumber is an exquisite, peaceful occurrence—not unlike this body's final reclining, and being emptied into rearranged particle-waves of space.

When our form dies, we cycle back to our Source, and the pure Energy all matter is made of—just like every night in falling asleep, we let go of the body-mind and relax into That … And come each daybreak, we are gracefully stirred by the same Force now dawning, everywhere inside us and all around our room.

Night or day, in sleeping or moving about, in this life and beyond, our overall Awakening is our resting assured of being home.

* * *

There are all kinds of very serious stories we may be wrapped up in—the ones featuring our personal history, our habits, situations, so-called deficiencies and paths of self-development we wish we could practice more ardently and consistently … Again, we can't help it. Obsessing about ourselves is what we have learned and come to think of as normal in our culture; and when we're so engrossed in the "plots" of our lives, we think they're telling us everything. What luck to be so mistaken!

What luck to be compassionately amused by all we think needs fixing, and the extra willpower we're convinced we have to muster. The ways we puff ourselves up in our posturing, in trying to prove ourselves and secure our place in the "scheme" of things—all these give us a chance to chuckle at the human comedy. And just like watching our children at play (and how seriously they take their roles), we *can* laugh at ourselves when we see things from the point of view of our true Identity.

As far as the roles we assume as adults, we can embrace and even perfect them, play them as best we're able. We can put attention on our jobs and being more prosperous, on fulfilling our potential as husbands and wives, parents, artists, athletes, you name it—while simultaneously listening to our innermost, sage advice. This might suggest looking at our lives as if we could reflect on them from a very old age, to see how much of value our fretting, and plotting, positioning and preening have really gotten us; and then, living accordingly, *now.*

To not take ourselves so seriously may be much less interesting for many people. The mere mention of surrender sounds passive, lifeless, terrifying even, especially if it's confused with any form of self-denial or resignation. Many might insist, "I need to be motivated, 'work' on myself, maximize my personal powers and maybe even teach others how to do so; only this will get me excited and provide my life with a meaningful legacy."

As I view it, any version of a real "success story" has, as its central theme, the discovery of our *core*-truth, our essence. In such a tale, our trust and letting go are anything but passionless—as we recognize What is being given way to and the energy of heartfelt giving This instills in us.

* * *

Failing to love is the only real failure, and reversing this trend is the surest sign of true success.

* * *

VII

Great Spirit, Origin of the wind, healer of wounds, voice and ears of my devotion, Who is birthing and deathing every sight and every sound: I lay my head down in your infinite Lap, and with it, all my problems and fears—not knowing what the future holds, not needing it to be a certain way … And if I do prefer any particular outcome, this too is best envisioned through these Eyes of yours by which I see, beholding You everywhere I look.

* * *

How good, to let the universal Spirit, or "breath of God" in everyone, influence the particulars in our lives— letting *any* moment be Spiritual practice—be an expression of our heart's most expansive reach! When this becomes what we're about, we bear witness to our core-truth, Who we *are*, really—the love that's breathing in and out our Oneness.

This is distinguishable, in my view, from relegating "spiritual" to out-of-body experiences, the paranormal, or ascending to some other dimension and away from the here and now of our earthly life. Some even speak of "spirits" as disembodied beings who exist in other realms and somehow affect what goes on in this world … And there may be other planes of existence which transcend this one and in some way influence it; I have no idea. What I am sure of, is wherever we live, in whatever time or place, the *All that is is present.* How could it be otherwise?

* * *

If one is moved to practice things like positive thinking, affirmations or visualizations, it's good to remember they exist in the truth of our being, with the truth of our being not dependent on them. We don't need to bring to mind certain images, ideas or ideals; or be captivated by auras, apparitions or vibrations to get to Where we already are. And any of these activities are fine, as long as we know they are temporary snapshots of What is in superabundance—before, during and after a thought, or feeling appears and disappears … Best, then, that anything made into a ritual or a practice defers to What everything exists in and flows out of, even the opposite of what we're affirming or visualizing.

It's true, maintaining a vision of the truth in the mind is a most wondrous capacity, and there are many accounts of people who attribute growth and healing to such means … This being said, it's good to understand how seeking purely positive thoughts, and excluding their contrasts, can assume (even subtly) that our true Nature only exists when a certain mind-form is occurring, or when a special technique is applied, or when inspiring moments are happening or we feel a certain way.

When any mental imagery dims or vanishes, or when uplifting appearances go away (as all appearances will), our essence is still here!—our being at home in God always our *most essential* truth. What greater affirmation is there than this—what greater impetus for our love?

* * *

In any moment, we may be moved in a sublime and potent manner by the infinite Radiance in and around us, and venerate This by any and all activities we consider sacred. As far as experiences go, these are most beautiful ones, and if they occur, we might feel different than we did before. But sooner or later, these or any other thoughts, and feelings and moments will fade, will change, as every occurrence does ... How perfect, then, that our Source-connection isn't confined to so-called meaningful events we might want to capture, recapture or enshrine.

The breadth of God's spirit in us isn't determined by, or limited to anything happening in time and space. And even if in our forgetfulness, we have apparently left our true home, we get to apparently return in our remembrance and know we have never been away.

* * *

If it seems we have forgotten Who we are, still, nothing is lacking—just as discovering our true Self is nothing to gain. We may think there is deficit or attainment, but those are limited views, ideas, and believing what's Real is defined by them, or only confined to the highlights of our experience or the pinnacle of our aspirations.

While we may appear, at times, to lose awareness of This, Consciousness itself can't be lost (even if we imagine it's like a game of "hide-and-go-seek") ... In truth, *It's* always here, seeing through us, vibrating in our every cell and coursing through our veins—no matter how caught up in things we can sometimes be, or how we might enjoy any game of peek-a-boo.

* * *

What many are searching for is nearer than near, closer than close, most commonplace and beyond belief—in going anywhere or being still … There is no way to arrive here, to realize this, until we get that we're presently There and presently It.

And just like the love parents can't help having for their children—it's ingrained, *most* primal, in hearts so full and spilling out!

* * *

I pray to be open even as I say, "No" to someone, or set the boundaries for my children I sometimes need to. While saying, "No," and standing strong and resolute in any moment, am I being considerate of the other person, and who that one really is—however he or she acts or appears to be?

If the "tough love" of being firm or taking a stand makes me so narrow-minded or stubborn that I can't begin to put myself in another's shoes; or even worse, is used as an excuse to intimidate, humiliate or invalidate anyone—may I be forever stopped in my tracks. Tough love isn't love at all, if I'm not willing to invite another into the tenderness at my core.

* * *

When we feel the need to address our children's behavior, or take away some of their privileges as is sometimes necessary, the most important thing is how we do this. Can we let our essential truth show through the structures we create, our firm tones of speech and any discipline we impose—always keeping our children's well-being and maturation in the foreground of our attention? This means being mindful of any tendency in us, as parents, to be on a "power trip," and needing to be right and in control at all costs … When our guidance tips too heavily in this direction, we may forget what our parenting is meant to serve—like helping our offspring choose for themselves what's most beneficial, and how good it is to be a responsible and caring human being. What better way than by being this way ourselves, and to lead by example.

Even when we might get cranky and out of sorts with our kids (or they with us), the quick returning to our acknowledged intimacy lets us learn about forgiveness, making amends and letting bygones be gone. This is how our love is strengthened: by being continually reminded how much our children mean to us; and likewise, how much we mean to them, in terms of helping to fortify their inclination to love.

So, as we guide our children as best we can, we also know their lives may head in directions we wouldn't necessarily choose as our own. Our true support, then, encourages them to really listen to what's inside their hearts as they follow them—to trust Where this openness comes from and leads, as the unavoidable process of trial and error occurs.

* * *

There's a tendency in all of us to resist letting go—of relationships ending, or when someone has died or when our kids start to grow up and become different than they were. It's OK; we do get attached. There's this idea we shouldn't and that we ought to feel a certain way, or be able to accept and let go, no matter what. We can just let go of this idea of letting go—really!

This not only goes for people we like, but also for those we quite honestly don't, or with whom we're upset. We might not like having unpleasant feelings about someone, thinking we "should" be able to immediately release these. Well, let's face it, sometimes it doesn't work out that way, as it's so human to be bothered by other humans. We can admit to this, and any annoyance, or irritation or indignation, and allow what's happening to happen … Real letting go, then, is letting *be*—a love that bears being OK with not being OK.

In regard to our children, if we fight against their growing up and making choices for themselves, we're denying them the room to be how they are, to discover things for themselves and learn from their mistakes. This is hard for many of us as parents, just as it was for our parents during our growing pains. We're smart, then, to extend to our kids what we would to ourselves—the biggest space to be with whatever any of us is feeling and experiencing.

In being open, we can be open-ended toward whatever any moment brings, including our being attached, resisting change and sometimes appearing unlike how we think we should be. This openness reflects the love and trust of home, which houses everything and everyone having likable *and* unlikable qualities—everything and everyone having a beginning, an end and countless periods of transition.

When we really understand that every form is transforming and every event passing, we're more likely to let changes be ... Fond memories do have a certain sweetness to them we can savor; but if our fixation on the past runs us, becoming more predominate than our truth-telling, then we're somehow resisting the inevitable ebb and flow of people, things and situations. We have forgotten the natural way of Life if we don't accept someone's freedom to move on, or when we have difficulty facing the body's getting old and dissolving. That's why it's good to be realistic about how things are—always in flux, coming and going, whether we like it or not ... Thank goodness it all takes place Where it does, and This is where we live.

* * *

At any moment, we might encounter someone with whom we've been at odds— someone, perhaps, deserving of our most sincere apologies. And perhaps, there are also those from whom we yearn to hear the same, "I'm truly sorry, please forgive me."

How any of us acts can lead to varying degrees of upset, disappointment or regret; and we can easily feel let down, perplexed and saddened by how events in and around us unfold. There are, thus, many ways we might experience our hearts breaking— which, if the *whole* truth be told, is perfect for the sake of the mending and the ever-Presence of true healing.

* * *

I would like these writings to be ones a person can turn to, open anywhere, at anytime, and receive the basic message. These are the communications I find most helpful—that are getting to the point, over and over again.

So, I am meditating on our core-truth, our being home right now and always, and expressing this in various and repeated ways, knowing how we can keep replaying the same unhappy story in our heads or in our daily lives. And in my own case (and for most people, I'd surmise) constant reminders have been useful—to assist in opening eyes, when conditioned behavior may be continually closing them.

Most likely, there will be a wide range of reception and opinions about what's presented here, as there is to everything, written or otherwise. Some people will be indifferent; some will agree with parts and disagree with others, wishing perhaps, they could be stated in different ways. Some will praise some of what I say, or all of it, and might say it is profound and inspirational; and some won't get what's meant until later; and others, never at all. And some people will simply disagree, and say this is not what they believe in, or what their ministers, or teachers or favorite books say ... Such is the play of the Universe, where a lot of points of view are occurring and many voices speaking.

The most important matter is what rings true in us, and this may be in response to one word in this book, one phrase or the whole thing ... Perhaps, a deep chord is struck while listening to someone else, or in being with a loved one on his or her deathbed, or during the birth of one's child or while gazing at the eternal elegance of a flower in a field ... Whatever it takes!

* * *

VIII

The ways of the world push and pull at us to be experts at what we do, and somebody special who has credentials and things to show off. That's fine as far as that goes, and all that goes with it—feeling confident, or proud or praiseworthy about anything we do.

Yet even if a person has vast knowledge, and the capacity to manage and direct people and situations, what good is this without a generous heart easily given to great joy and humility? Even if someone is supremely confident, creative, eloquent, able to fix complicated things, help cure diseases, understand the workings of anyone's mind or predict future events, what then? These abilities don't necessarily translate into a happiness brimming with what's priceless inside—a spirited glow not requiring advanced, much less superhuman means.

Alas, there is a blessed undoing coming from our depths, where nobody is special *and* everyone is; where no credentials are needed, as we stand naked in even the finest clothes—all revealed, all equal, in our Maker's eyes … And yes, each of us is given unique capabilities, strengths and weaknesses, and play various roles. Still, we're all in God, and That in us—however we appear, and succeed, or fail, rise or fall.

* * *

As human expressions of God's totality, we are but a portion of This spectrum of possibility. Whatever capabilities each of us is given, extraordinary or not, we can never know or control everything … While taking charge of our lives in the ways we're able, and responsibility for the things we need to, there *will* be times not turning out the way we'd like, and *much* that remains a mystery and beyond our power to grasp or manipulate.

The design of the universe, and the Intelligence behind it, clearly supercedes how we might think this, or any world should be ideally or could will it so. We constantly come up against the limits of human comprehension, and are easily confounded by unpredictability and apparent randomness—especially in regard to the suffering we see and experience, and all that overwhelms our sensibilities, or appears inhumane, insane or evil.

Some people, when facing the unknown and what only the whole scope of the Big Picture can reveal, might be bewildered, but OK with their "wires" being scrambled; some who may be dismayed, disgruntled or made more cynical; and some who feel mostly anxious, distraught or lost. And others can't help being brought to their knees in awe, confessing perhaps, that "God works in mysterious ways"—with the capacity to appear paradoxical, and even unlike how we imagine that One should be, or act, or answer our prayers exactly as we would wish.

The Totality is *most* vast and all-inclusive, and nothing our minds can completely figure out or grab a hold of; and greater, certainly, than any idea or theory we can pigeonhole, tailor to the expediency of our beliefs or personal desires. This, to me, points to the greatest profundity, and the reason for letting any confines and confusion of mind and emotion rest in their Divine underpinnings, and our true Reality, in fact … We can, at least, be smart enough to understand this: What transcends our mind's grasp will always be so; what else, then, but to let be and embrace the Mystery—and in the process, see through any belief-system which may be intentionally or unintentionally trying to pin down and limit what, in truth, cannot be (and can, in fact, give rise to all kinds of divisions and conflicts—within ourselves and between each other—which is common when any one idea, theory or ideology is pitted against another).

And yes, the appearance of separation and all our struggles—*everyone and everything*, are arising out of and cycling back into God. And however our world may seem, we can *open wide* to What's creating us, living and transforming us. We can call this opening, this letting be, love; we can call it faith or settling into being home.

Whatever we name it, it is a most natural response when we see what happiness, what peace, there is here.

* * *

When our pursuit for a fulfilling life is all about "me and mine," we can appear estranged from our essence, even to the extent of using people and things for personal or collective ends exclusively, despite what ill-will or harm these actions might cause. And how evident this is, when our selfishness turns love (no matter how cleverly masqueraded) into possessiveness, and attempts to manipulate, control and dominate others.

To the degree this ("sin," as some would call it) is going on, a vicious cycle ensues, as we seek for genuine happiness in ways that only push it further away from us— by keeping us perpetually self or group obsessed, and blind to the Source of our completeness ... Whatever it's called, the suffering resulting from this mistake is part of the times we've been born into and what we continue to create. We read about it every day in the newspaper and it's on TV every night—often hidden behind fake smiles, insincere gestures and trying to keep up appearances.

Even in terms of our religions (and despite the word meaning to "re-legion," or bring together and reunite), there can be the same signs of power-seeking, exclusion and megalomania occurring in worldly-minded realms ... When we identify so heavily with our ideologies, our side's story, and are so zealous in our convictions, all hell can break loose. If we're convinced we represent all that's virtuous and righteous and somebody else doesn't, then the ferocity of these delusions can be extreme and sometimes violent; we might think we have the perfect excuse—in spite of the message of benevolence, pure-hearted worship and humankind's oneness from which our beliefs may have originated. Isn't this one of history's greatest and most tragic ironies?—how our religions have been the justification for so many conflicts and wars.

Even in supposedly benign and well-intentioned ways: Trying to make others believe the way we do can create great divisiveness; and even if we're not literally at war, "my creed and what it promises is superior to yours," gets played out all the time ... Understandable, given our egocentricity and greed, even in "God's name;" and good, therefore, to recognize how this hardens us, corrupts us—and gracefully, paves the way of our downfall and the chance to be brought to our knees—cracked open and repentant.

* * *

We're all unqualifiedly related to our common Origin, and therefore, to one another; this is *most* true … And while we may suffer in so many ways from falsely believing there's no such thing as real togetherness—as the Oneness underlying our multiplicity—this is a way to tell the difference between our essential truth and our essential lie.

* * *

If it's just in our minds or in our speech or actions, it's good to see how judgmental we are. It's true, we need to decide which way to turn the car and the best ways to teach our children. And we're constantly making comparisons about what foods to buy, the best candidate to vote for, the right person to marry; the list is endless. Part of being in this world is about choosing one thing over another, following through on a choice, weighing options and gauging situations in order to know how to proceed. Our lives are naturally given to having preferences, and letting these influence what we do.

On the other hand, being judgmental can take the form of, "I shouldn't be thinking these thoughts, I wish I had better ones;" or, "I'm more evolved than this person, but not as good as that person;" or, "I've got what you don't, or I wish I had what you do." Each of us has our own version of how the judgmental mind works, and how pompous and critical we can be; or on the flip side of this, how full of self-doubt and self-condemnation we can be.

There's a tendency to stay stuck in our interpretation of things, and how we're sizing up a person or a situation. We often rush to judge, and define people with quick opinions and attitudes like, "I'm better than you or worse than you;" or, "You should be like me or different than you are;" or, "I wish I were as lovable as I used to be." ... We're quick to worry about "measuring up," and how we stand in whatever "pecking order" we imagine for ourselves. Being judgmental like this is an example of our narrow-mindedness, and keeps us stuck in things like suspicion, shame and envy.

As opinions and comparisons spontaneously pop up, it's good to know they're a result of our conditioning and what usually starts taking hold in childhood—when, to a great extent, we can't help receiving what's passed on to us—like being overly critical, biased, and prone to jumping to conclusions and making mis-"takes" about people and events ... If we're intending to grow up, we can let our truth-telling fine-tune our attention and soften any hardening around our hearts, so our judgmental tendencies are seen for what they are and we are forgiven for being "all too human." And with even a moment of this clarity and compassion, any unnecessary constraints we put upon ourselves can be recognized and released, and we can choose something different— different than what even the most conditioned behavior and debilitating habits might otherwise dictate.

* * *

Even though our minds are depositories of all our thought-habits (including fears and desires, false assumptions and accusations we've inherited or concocted), the light of Awareness has no difficulty shining over any of it, through any of it, and letting us see from a thoroughly revealing perspective.

This much is clear, then: The mind is not our enemy, nor our savior, and it doesn't need to be overcome or worshipped ... It is, thankfully, a handy tool for "thinking things through," making the choices we must in our lives, *and* a vehicle for Consciousness to look out of and, thus, our chance to reflect on our real and true brightness.

It only takes a flashing moment!—for the mind to face itself and recognize its Nature, awake in the vastness and splendor of the view ... We realize, then, we *are* this Awareness—this Seeing—above and beyond and radiating on what is seen.

* * *

IX

Responding to our core-truth has a certain ease to it, just like falling in love with someone, and not having to try and remember that he or she touches us inside. When we're moved in such a way, we can't help opening.

And a natural effort, in the sense of fortitude, stick-to-itiveness and "giving our all" goes along with this ease; as does the gaining of physical, mental and emotional strength ... Our simplest, purest devotion engenders these in the broadest sense: We have the greatest courage and determination, "have heart," when we're willing to tell the complete truth and stay true to that—true to ourselves; and whether, in any moment, we feel strong or weak, find love easy to express or not, this sincerity and its resolve can remain steadfast. Then, in terms of whatever else we might be going for, there's little at stake, really, since our primary aim has already found its mark.

* * *

It's my sense, that finding the Source of genuine happiness happens at the same time as we're being found ... There's a commingling of our intention to discover "It," and the Grace sparking this interest and helping us consummate our deepest desire. Maybe just a sniff at first; then, at some point, our inmost fragrance begins to be the air we breathe, wherever we are.

For some of us, our dissatisfaction may intensify. We start to see things that once gave us moments of pleasure, distraction or excitement no longer doing it. "There must be something more to life," we might ask, or a way to find what we're really looking for.

Isn't this the crux of what's going on—the gnawing sense of dislocation from one's well-being and inner peace, and the crying out to be rejoined? ... How wonderful, then, absence *can* make us grow fonder, especially for home. And even more so, how magnificent that we're already here!

* * *

It strikes me, that times of doubt and confusion, feeling lost and stuck, indecisive and fickle, are invaluable in turning us inside out.

When finally, we realize we're traveling down familiar dead-end roads and quickly running out of options, we just might see there's nowhere else to turn, and nowhere we'd rather be than the spacious caverns of our heartland.

Then, we might understand: It's all been leading to this, and nothing can stand in the way of our unearthing and nothing is left standing that must inevitably fall.

* * *

In wanting to remedy one's discontent, or escape having to look at its causes, there's a tendency to become addicted to what we think will help us feel better (or to what numbs us, so we won't feel much at all). Many people are self-medicating, and searching for ways to be comfortable, or consoled, energized or transcendent-like in their own skin.

And it's not just with things like drugs and alcohol. We can be hooked on any number of substances and activities—on money and luxury, power and control, food and sex, recognition and fame and adrenaline rushes of all kinds, including peak inspirational experiences. Like we've talked about before: Any fixation on trying to satisfy the individual or collective entity alone, or seeking the constant via what is only temporary, keeps us looking for happiness in all the wrong places. As obvious as it sounds, it bears repeating: What we're really looking for is never found in anything incapable of providing it.

This isn't a weakness or a defect in one's character, as we're only being human in wanting to feel more alive, or relaxed or less bored, even if we imagine it's through getting "high" on whatever we do. The problem is, of course, any drug not only fails to truly fulfill us (or keep hidden what cries for revelation), but the side effects are very costly. The initial pleasant feelings are very short-lived; they are quickly followed by increased discomfort and craving, greater excesses, toxicity, depleted energy, isolation, wrong decisions, as well as the possibility of debt, injury, jail and death.

However it occurs for any of us, we drop our bad habits when they've sufficiently worn themselves out—when we experience both the limitations and even intolerable pain of our behavior patterns, *and* finally being able to act accordingly. This happens when it does; and for many of us, there is a definite sense of Grace intervening then—a "higher Power," or light going on in us and illuminating our life-directions. Whatever we call it, and through whatever circumstances it takes place, This is discovered to be the real transforming, healing Force. And usually, we'll only go with this flow when our futile pursuits and self-inflicted misery leave us at last with little or no resistance.

* * *

The best way to deal with any unhealthy behavior is to replace it with what's truly healthy. Value this shift in priorities and honor it enough, and our actions begin to show that. We stop doing things which keep us foggy in the head, poisoning our own body and its surroundings and contaminating our relationships.

Waking up from these kinds of nightmares has the feel of being mercifully shaken from our delusions and self-deception. From out of nowhere, it dawns on us, either slowly or in a split second: Now's the time to change our ways and partake in the Substance of the mercy—by opening to and loving just like it.

* * *

The most fundamental dis-ease, and a contributing factor in many specific diseases, is the belief (be it subconscious, or subtle or blatantly nagging), that we're alienated or even severed altogether from our core-contentment; and all we're left with, then, are these forms we incessantly try to please, while being hardened and reactive toward what we dislike. This is one way to describe the stress in our lives.

And, it is well known now how this contributes to many ailments. Heart disease, especially (and some cancers, it is now being discovered), are made more likely by mental and emotional tension, and the resulting behavior patterns and destructive habits. And, really, the likelihood of any illness increases when our dis-ease lowers the substances in the brain and immune system helping us stay well or heal ourselves … If we notice, the list of stress-related maladies grows with each passing year of research and study.

What goes a long way toward optimal health, and healing the primary dysfunction, is our commitment to the whole truth, or true "holiness," about ourselves—our innate Wholeness. This gives our overall wellness a much greater chance of happening, as the natural curative powers present in openness, ease of being and equanimity work best when we let them—when we're inclined to *be* this way.

And it's certain, all of us experience physical illness, ups and downs in thoughts and feelings, and the body's unavoidable aging and passing away. This is how the current of Life is—with forms "coming ashore" for a time and then ebbing back to their Origin … So, even as we face medical challenges, including those impossible to overcome, there remains a truly healthy perspective and attitude—stemming from a trust, or faith, rooted in the most thorough truth-telling—whatever shape we appear to be in and however long we have as a body-mind.

* * *

There are those who say we've been plagued, doomed even, since the beginning of human time, by the fact that we have the capacity, even the propensity, to turn away from our connection to God, or actually presume no such bond exists at all.

Some call this a "fall from grace," some say it's our "original sin," which we've inherited from our earliest ancestors and are condemned to commit at any time, given our conditioned tendencies to do so ... And some, myself included, do see many of us appearing lost, and seeking genuine happiness and inner peace—not yet realizing the abundance of these in the home we're *always* in—that's always in us. When we *do* wake up to Where we are, we can be certain of being anything but plagued, or doomed or condemned—certain that Grace is ever-present.

So, however we view the human condition, and our varying degrees of ignorance, bad decisions, misplaced priorities and loveless behavior, any of it can be swiftly consumed when we're turned inside out by What's *everywhere* we turn, and therefore, impossible to be separate from—the Life-Spark that is our heart's pulsation, its flame, and eternity's home within our ashes.

* * *

It's good to be pierced by an intensity of insight—of how we, in any way, sabotage what we know to be true by valuing anything else more than it—by selling out.

This wake-up call is best treated as a dear friend and one never to be gotten rid of … Whenever I engage in any form of Self-betrayal, or deny the love and happiness of my essence for the sake of some other habit or desire, it's good that this (or any variation of hard-heartedness) pains me, and serves to crack me open to my reunion … However, poignant or harsh, abrupt or slow, this is a most blessed, valuable kind of pain.

* * *

Answering the call of our true Nature may not appear easy because of our conditioned thinking, behavior patterns and the times in which we're living. We might assume we're just these people struggling to get by, or trying to fill up perceived voids in our lives or climb whatever "ladder of success" we're driven to.

But again, all of this is our greatest ally, and the perfect opportunity to find out the consequences of buying into the lie—that who we might think we are, strive to be and hope to achieve is more relevant, more important, than Who we are *already and always*, in truth—more rewarding than giving way to This and seeing our amazement and gratitude thrive in us ... And however painfully loud any reminders might be (to not believe the lie), redemption is an easily recognized shift in attention, in priorities, and a welcoming in the heart— thanks to the Spirit that so becomes us, no matter who or what we choose to become.

* * *

Consider the miracle occurring in every moment: We're riding on this giant ball of rock and water that's floating and spinning in midair, amongst other planets and stars too numerous to count!

And, by the same Presence is each of us being breathed, heart-pumped and our every brainwave and cell imbued ... Such is the ultimate "mind-blower"— What's so big It has no end *and*, at the same time, is immeasurably small—the space we abide in wherever we go and kneel down in to hear our soul's secret being told.

Whatever name we give to it, our soul *is* our essence, our innermost, our heart of hearts, the core of us that's most vast and love-filled. Here, we're most intimately joined with God—in a body-mind for a time and as a soul forever ... No accumulated amount of remembrance or good works is necessary to fulfill this union, nor can any of our mundane thoughts or difficult circumstances ever remove us from it. *And*, what a beautiful thing and part of our experience to "come back home," when it seems we've been everywhere else but there.

* * *

All is arising from the one Source, and multiplied beyond trillions and trillions. Thus, we are One, while in This being many—each of us from God, in God and back into That.

What a moment, then, when we peer all the way inside and see our true face is no face at all, as well as every one we look at everywhere we go—seeing the immaculate emptiness and What's *all*-pervasive.

As a result, we get to choose what we've been given to find—after perhaps appearing blind to our convergence and Where we've been all along.

* * *

There are some people who are intuitively certain of being led by a "writer" or "director" behind the "script" of their lives moving them toward certain destinations. And equally so, is there not the individual's power of choice, as fundamental in navigating this human journey?

It's clear to me, whether we go where we do because of "fate," or "free will" or a combination of the two, we can walk within our infinite heart, even as we might be in the dark about what's around the next bend or exactly how we got there … We can simply love, can look to our deepest truth, no matter what's going on.

And maybe there *is* a higher Intelligence with a basic notion or even a distinct plan for each of us before we leave the womb. Or just maybe there is no such thing, in order for our Source to know what it's like being surprised—by what means bring about what ends, without knowing ahead of time what these are.

Whatever happens, my strongest inkling is that each of our destinies, and our capacity to create and choose, are one and the same Being taking unique shape in every life, and experiencing all the ways of being us.

* * *

An integral part of the human experience is about seeing what results occur from whatever we do. Sometimes we know immediately what these effects and consequences are, sometimes we don't or we're unsure, and sometimes we understand much further down the road.

I look at responsibility as our ability to respond to situations in ways we know have true worth. This occurs when it does—when we begin to live on the basis of what's *really* important to us. Whether we're children or adults, each of us is at a unique place in this process of growing up.

Maturing, in this sense, is about being drawn to the "fire" of truth-telling, tending its warmth amid all we do and letting it burn up any refusal to live as such. We can see, then, how this regard for What's at our depths fuels a basic integrity, decency and respect for others; and that these come through in specific ways—like keeping our promises and commitments, supporting our families and communities, taking care of our bodies, planet earth, and helping our friends in need.

Bottom line is, being home implies being responsible for our love—to embody it, to "own it," and utilize the nurturing qualities we're given, in our giving to ourselves and others. And I'm convinced we're the happiest when we're this way, even toward what appears unlovable … After all, the Totality includes all of us who might do bad and stupid things; that's why anyone can still be blessed and treated with dignity: We are always one with God, regardless of sometimes not knowing it or acting like it.

* * *

There is a natural dedication that develops if we sincerely want to be good at something, like a musical instrument, or a new language or occupation, for example. And maintaining a certain focus on our learning, and persisting in our practice of it result from this dedication, and are essential to the educational process and becoming more accomplished, whatever our interests or goals might be.

In the case of discovering our true Self, one could call this a goal; but what's great about this goal is it's realizable in the heartbeat of every here and now … This might seem to magnify and become more consistent over time, and our future moments may arrive with seemingly greater epiphanies and inner harmony. Or, perhaps, we notice that nothing special is happening, or only seems to be, intermittently.

Unmistakably, then, being attuned to our core-resonance can come about and affect us in varying ways and degrees; and like all occurrences in time and space, they appear and disappear in every conceivable manner … In any event, and no matter what, we're already complete—as That who is living us and being our home.

And how perfect, that we can hear this truth in any instant, and there are no rehearsals required for this awakening "chime" to ring in us, nothing amplified we need to feel, no level of performance to maintain or anyone's approval to seek ... There *is* most wonderfully, the wooing of our hearts and the ceaseless returning of this favor in kind.

* * *

Each of us has the opportunity to find
What's closer than any ritual, or practice,
method or path could ever hope to take us.

So, as we savor moments of being still, and
quiet and aware of the breath of Life, as
well as any song of Spirit-praise—it's
clear: *This* fills the air—whether we're as
motionless as the eye of a hurricane, or
exhilarated by the storm's force or tossed
and tattered by whatever it kicks up.

* * *

Living according to our essential Nature doesn't need to gauge itself with any ideal measure of tranquility, self-esteem, acknowledgment or longevity; nor must we try and hush up or shut out what may seem contradictory to our realization or to interfere with it … There's nothing and no one to live up to, nothing to be transcended or heightened feeling-state to hone.

Likewise, every moral code we might believe in or live under, best answers to love's most direct and urgent plea—love's simplest expression … This melts any need for strict "shoulds," or hype or restrictive commands from an authority figure/superego standing over us in our minds, from church pulpits or in the sky.

* * *

Discerning intelligence is sometimes a necessary act of love—to say, "Yes" to something or someone and, "No" to the alternative, and being appropriately cautious and skeptical about the people and situations warranting it.

And real intelligence also knows it's OK *not* knowing what to say, "Yes" or, "No" to and that our best interests lay bare in the open heart—where uncertainty and skepticism can relax, having found a home.

Here, our taking care of business and handling our affairs, our being realistic and pragmatic, are given a great purpose—to help provide and care for any of us in our embodiment ... And even if this should seem difficult, or have its ups and downs, we can *still and always* attend to What's all right and most Real, in any case. To realize this is our greatest, lasting fortune, and the firmest foundation on which to live.

* * *

In terms of any decisions in our lives, like where to live, where to send our kids to school, which job to take or doctor to choose: We can do things like going over the pros and cons of any choice we're faced with, and adding up both sides of the issue. We can sit with the whole thing for a while and see what's revealed. At some point, we must act; and it will either be from the pros outweighing the cons, or a "gut level" kind of thing—what feels right and best serves our life's objectives.

But, as we also know, our thoughts, and feelings and circumstances can change, being one way one day, and one way the next. What we once thought was a sure thing or a done deal can fall flat, and people we trusted or held in high esteem may fail to live up to those expectations. All of this is imploring us to follow a much more reliable and trustworthy principle—one that's unshakable amid the shifting tides of this world.

So, when we've made a mistake, chosen poorly or change our mind about a specific decision, it's *OK*.

What's preeminent is in plain sight, regardless, and
Where everything takes place and ends up.

* * *

When any of us hurts another, it might not appear as bad as someone on the daily news who's committed a most heinous act; but let's face it, we can be just as malicious in our minds, our emotions or slips of the tongue … In subtle or not so subtle ways, and throughout our lives, we can be doing harm in our imaginations, our casual speech, innuendoes, sarcasm and body language.

It's also certain, further insight and the lessons that come in time are always needed to see more clearly and act more maturely. And how else do we grow up, truly?—but through the repenting of our lapses from what does us the most good.

Furthermore, if we tell the truth about the common Origin of our next breath, we see that our circle of relations is larger than we might have presumed. Its circumference, in fact, reaches far and wide, *really* far and wide. Our web is spun in more directions than we can possibly imagine; and there's no question, when we hurt someone, physically, emotionally or in our thoughts, we're impacting ourselves at the same time.

Therefore, if there are people in our lives we have wronged or who have wronged us—who can't forgive us or we have trouble forgiving—this is the perfect chance to pay homage to our higher Power. This is a love truly worth worshipping, and one never diminished by any of our loveless ways—letting us forgive ourselves for not forgiving, and extend, and request and receive needed apologies.

* * *

In considering moments in my life I regret, on the one hand, there are plenty of them. If only I knew in the past what I know now, I might have treated someone or some situation in a different manner—making all the difference in what I'm now feeling remorseful about. If only I didn't have the habits and tendencies keeping me confused in the head and narrow in my understanding, I could have made wiser choices, better kept my word and offered kinder gestures. But I didn't; I was at whatever stage of maturity I was, and at times, being as dumb and foolish as a person can be.

So … Any of us can bring whatever we might feel guilty about into the room we're sitting in, and the one deep within us. Here, there is complete freedom to feel whatever we're feeling—a Source-communing sanctuary of such welcoming, that forgiveness comes as naturally as breathing in and breathing out.

In here, we know our regret can serve us, as learning from the past is vital, in order to stop repeating patterns of unhappiness … And we're also reminded, that no matter what has happened and how ignorant and cruel we've been, the present is the only time we're in. We can do absolutely nothing about the past, except create a better future by how we are now; and while we're served by understanding what's previously occurred, the past is not worth fixating on and needlessly rehashing. Realizing this is at the heart our release—our conversion to love and a gift of Grace that lets us.

* * *

Who I am is not confined to my age, my culture or history; nor any thought, emotion, bodily condition, self-image, belief, occupation, partner or event. Who I *am* began before all these ever happened and will continue forever after me.

In giving way to my essence, or telling the whole truth about myself, I'm handed a magnifying glass that brings every aspect of my personal or group identity into sharper focus. But rather than fighting the ones I don't like, or making idols of the ones I do, better to let them fuel my interest in looking homeward and through the eyes seeing from there. This is preferable to obsessing about my conditioned tendencies and their stories, which only binds me tighter to the belief that they represent my entirety.

Our Creator has fashioned the ego/persona, in both individual and collective guises, and knows it for what it is—knows the illusion of trying to find true happiness through glorifying it, changing it, polishing it or suppressing it. And it's my experience, we won't drop the weight of our illusions until they have gotten sufficiently heavy, *and* we begin to

fathom a fathomless trust in Where we all float and
Where we all sink.

* * *

There are those who are convinced they have lived before this life, and some of their traits will re-form into another body after this one's gone. That could happen; I don't know. I know nothing about past lives or future ones. What is so for me is this: Whatever takes place, our *very Being* always was and will be, in this or any form, in this or any life.

And what about heaven? ... In the sense of what occurs after we leave this world, maybe we do enter a brightly lit space filled with ethereal, angelic energy and the auras of others who've also passed—both those we get to love and be loved by again, *and* those we may have hurt or been hurt by ... Perhaps, heaven, then, is just like what's possible right now—the chance to be so honestly eye to eye with our Maker that we can't help simply loving, *period*—including making amends, giving and receiving forgiveness, and beholding that we are, indeed, all God's children united in this Kingdom.

And to me, "hell," on earth, or anywhere or time, refers to the despair of believing that we (or others perceived to be unworthy) are cut-off from our common Origin and Sustenance, wholeness and happiness. This is like suffocating, gasping for the Life-breath of love, and sabotaging our rescue with debilitating habits which keep us in turmoil—beating ourselves up. And however full of illusions our beliefs might be, they can seem extremely real and devastating. As many have experienced, war *does* feel like hell, either in our hearts and minds, or among us.

Thankfully, our relationship to anyone or anything can be Spirit-filled, even if this planet is forever filled with difficulties, and with people who couldn't care less about what's being talked about in this book. Whether we know it or not, our timeless, celestial Nature is *here*, and irrevocably sewn in each of us—and not just someday, or "up there" or after our physical form dissolves.

In realizing this, we know both heaven and hell exist in What contains all polarities, no matter what the moment or circumstances are. Thus, when any of us is humbled, and even agonized by the failure to love, how perfect. Only then, can any hardening around our hearts be softened to receive our core-caress; and however one phrases it or considers it, this intimacy is key to our restoration, our salvation, and an enlightened way to be.

* * *

I imagine my daughter asking me one day, "So, daddy, where is heaven?"

After being so beautifully caught off guard like only a child's question can do, I hear myself saying something like, "Where do you suppose our every heartbeat begins and ends?"

And this sigh that just came out of me, from Where did its breath originate and empty back into?"

As Laina gazes inquisitively my way, I might exclaim, "Isn't this heavenly!? God deep inside us, and everywhere all around—just like the love you and I have for each other—the kind that's just as infinite and never dies."

* * *

XI

We don't need to dial into a finer, "light-body" energy in order to discover the truth about ourselves. Who we are, in Reality, permeates every ounce of space, and not just the "higher frequencies" of anyone or any place.

And even as the Radiance in and around this world might, at times, seem shrouded by how many people are being, this doesn't mean the Light exists to any lesser degree; it just means some pairs of eyes are playing the parts of closing or looking away.

As it's referred to here, the Light is not the denial of darkness, but That which envelops the entire spectrum of light and dark, and the contrasts of good and evil, difficult and easy, life and death, joyful and sad and so on. This is a luminescence beaming through it all, including being lost so we can be found.

* * *

Limitlessly more and equally less than who I might think I am, Who is actually reading these words and hearing any sound occurring now? Who is breathing, crying, laughing, being born and dying, in fact? And Who is even being a "somebody" without the slightest interest in what I'm trying to say?

While we may appear at times to fail miserably and go through all the unavoidable pains of this life, at rock-bottom, nothing can refute or taint our measureless fullness and true Identity.

* * *

In gazing into the eyes of anyone else, is there not the same gleam of Awareness looking out through both of you?

Likewise, a curiosity about our insides may lead us to What makes the world go 'round: the One beat reverberating in every heart.

Such an emergence and panoramic view!—waking us up—just like any morning from the previous night's dream that seemed most real.

* * *

These writings are not about being optimistic in any usual sense, which can be fleeting and easily deflated by difficult times or catastrophic events.

This world is one where pleasant feelings and unpleasant feelings fluctuate, based in large part on mental and emotional activity, personal situations and the daily news. We tend to feel upbeat or not, depending on the conditions of our lives or the world … What I'm pointing to is much more substantial than that—the Substance of which real trust/faith is made. This does make everything better, but it's not about having optimistic thoughts as opposed to pessimistic ones, or uplifting moments of belief followed by shaken ones. Both can spontaneously occur, often alternating back and forth; and like all such occurrences, they come and go. What holds it all, however, is always here and alive in us, in fact!

It's understandable, then, to have pessimistic feelings concerning the Middle East (and for much of the world). Things won't fundamentally change there, or anywhere, without a flood of awakening in many people; and it's true, on the surface this doesn't seem to be taking place … Still, a major shift can occur (and may actually be in the works); and for this to happen, as I see it, those involved must go deeper than usual optimism—to Where we are right now and in any moment, in essence—at home in temples of reverence and peace-making for us all.

And it's well and good to wish, and envision what we want to take place someday—to hope for the best, for what we feel we deserve and how we think our lives should be—knowing full well, that any of these can easily get stuck in the disappointment, despondency and dismay our heart's core-truth never does.

* * *

I'm free when I really see there's nothing to lose—understanding what's Real can't be lost. When I know Who I am is presently complete, I'm free of the fear of not getting what I want. What more could I desire that is greater than that?

When the love for my Wholeness engulfs me like this, it's never merely abstract or just a dream. Every one of us and everything about us *are waves inseparable from God's ocean.* Even what look to be limitations, sorrows and dilemmas are surrounded by nothing but This water.

Being free accepts that we'll be subject to distress, discouragement and people doing harmful things; these will always be part of the human realm. We live in a world where positive and negative, highs and lows, pleasure and hardship necessarily coexist. And because any form (as form) is bound to time and space, we aren't immune from what goes on here—including every body decaying, day by day and year by year, caught in the ongoing round of birth and death.

There's no getting around our physical mortality; and I get we're meant to face this head on, and look *all* the way into ourselves … The briefest take is liberating—of

the One unmasking the body-mind and any spatial or
temporal parameters.

* * *

Some people are certain they can have or be anything they want, as long as their intention is strong enough and they remove all the obstacles in their way. But what about all those people who haven't and never will? Even after countless workshops, therapy and intensely focused attention and willpower, many of their desires go unfulfilled.

And what about anyone you can think of who is disadvantaged or impaired in some way, through no fault of his or her own? If there were complete freedom and ability to create an ideal, personalized reality, don't you think more of those adversely impacted would have succeeded in fashioning something different for themselves?

It's true, some folks with mental and physical limitations embrace their situations—some are even thankful for them and able to rise above the adversity; but equally as many do not and will not … Think about your own life or anyone else you know. Even without extremely difficult circumstances to overcome, do you have everything you've ever wanted? I doubt it. And I don't buy the argument that we're somehow to blame for this state of affairs because we haven't tried hard enough or sufficiently transcended our impediments.

The point I'm making is this: Life is manifesting in all sorts of ways, and we are the vehicles through which our Creator is expressing Himself/Herself. People are going to be how they are. Some will be totally goal and achievement oriented, certain they have the utmost decision-making capacity—that whatever they set their minds to they can have or become. And for others, this is definitely not happening; or it seems to for specific periods of time, but not consistently.

Ultimately, even those experiencing difficulties or who seem to be failing are expressing aspects of What is. Whatever moves through us we'll do, we'll be, including the possible frustration in not getting everything we want and being how we've always been … As I view it, no matter what parts we play in the scheme of things, and amid whatever's going on, we are always being shown on the screen of the Big Picture—already and endlessly shined through, already and endlessly alright.

* * *

When I listen very carefully to my innermost voice, I can hear something like this: "Let your hand rest in the center of your chest (even if it's just in your imagination), and feel into the breathing, the skin and the beating heart. Allow your attention to go right into what you're feeling, and from Where you are created and sustained in every moment."

We don't need any concept of what this is, or have to try and get connected or struggle to be where our attention is, in the pulse of our being, "in God's hands"—this serenity that says it all.

* * *

Sharing any of this is a way to serve, not a rank or a means of gaining any kind of status. It's also the case, in all walks of life, people naturally assume different functions, according to the capabilities and preferences a person is given … So, while each of us is unique and playing certain parts, we *are* the same One, in truth—from That and in It. This is Where we dwell, and our spiritual life is best lived by honoring this principle, and to hold any position, especially that of a teacher or minister, as lightly as we would the most delicate feather.

Whatever our roles are, it's the sovereignty of our Source-union that matters; and in this domain we are best served by being lifelong students of love, where any of us can recognize another as oneself, as one Self … This realization isn't reserved for the prominent or even most "virtuous" few, and no culture or lineage has exclusive claims on it; nor is there any payoff, like being anointed with special privileges or prestige. It *is* about discovering What's alive in the tender crevices of our hearts, where everyone is equal and has access, no matter how ideal or imperfect our lives or this world may seem. This is good news, and our true privilege to witness and proclaim!

* * *

It is a precious gift and auspicious time we've been handed—to consciously be home in a variety of ways, unique to the individual and any here and now.

In any instant, each of us can be traced back to our Origin; so the question, "Who am I, really?" supplies its own answer and the ending of the search. What we are looking for *is* Who is looking and already found—presently and forever immanent. This overriding sense may arrive in ways we might describe as mystical, and ecstatic and full of blissful reverie; or simply as a tacit certainty of What's here, no matter what we're experiencing.

At other times, this love might be expressed without any corresponding Self-inquiry or other such reflection—just blessing whatever's happening, especially the ordinary things and the daily encounters with people ... An open heart is good enough; and our Grace-given chance to tap into the Wellspring where welcoming and acceptance, kindness and compassion, forgiveness and letting go are abundant. Here, the best solutions to life's many challenges are a lot easier to recognize.

And as always, without total honesty our selfishness can quickly rear its head, and what we feel passionately about or have as a purpose becomes just another "me first" story. Then, even the notion of Who we are is used to motivate ourselves, pump ourselves up, in order to get what we think we don't have … What do we hope to get, after all? What's missing, really?

* * *

Staring me in the face is a universe perfectly created, including all the cracks in the "glass" *and* our attempts to repair them … And what a marvelous thing to help cure the world's ills. I'm convinced the only way this can happen, truly, is by living in response to the inherent Perfection of this or any place.

When we're so moved, each of us can "show up" in our special manner. And while there are many sides to a crystal and ways for the Light to reflect, there is *only* this Radiance, this Eternity, behind it all—only God.

* * *

We always have the perfect material to work with. Heaven has hell to ordain with blessing, the clenched fist undone inside our opening hand.

* * *

What fortune to have this human incarnation to realize Who we really are— That from where we come, the Life-Force by which we are sustained and the Vastness awaiting our return …

What fortune, that everything we're discouraged by or think is dead inside is ground being tilled and readied for new life to grow …

What fortune to be cultivated in this never-ending landscape.

* * *

When my wife Minako and I are around our daughter Laina, we can't help being touched in our hearts by what's in hers, and exchanging glances filled with childlike exuberance and wonder.

The purity of Laina's love for Minako and me reaches deep inside us, and where the same devotion we have for her is most bountiful … Life's sweetest nectar is tasted here.

* * *

In the end and always, an open heart *is* good enough. It's all we need.

* * *

About the Author

I live in San Rafael, California with my wife Minako, our daughter Laina and Minako's son Lucas ... As well as sharing what's in <u>Being Home</u>, I am by profession, a Fitness Trainer and Yoga Instructor. I hold a B.A. degree in Philosophy from Pomona College, attended Harvard Divinity School, and have teaching credentials in Meditation, Yoga and Personal Training.

Contact via: www.heartstruth.net

978-0-595-42465-8
0-595-42465-1